PETER PAUL
RUBENS

TEXT BY

JULIUS S. HELD

Department of Fine Arts, Barnard College,
Columbia University, New York

THE LIBRARY OF GREAT PAINTERS

Portfolio Edition

HARRY N. ABRAMS *Publishers* NEW YORK

MILTON S. FOX, Editor • WALTER NEURATH of Thames & Hudson Inc., Supervisor of Color Plates

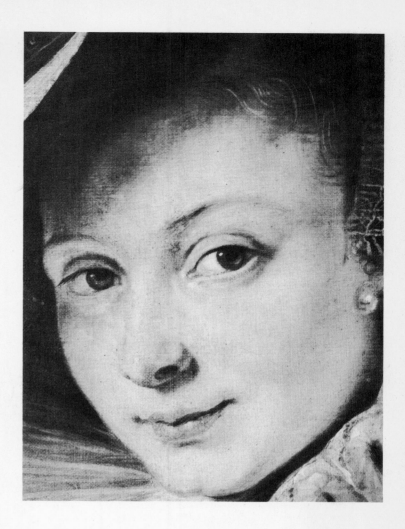

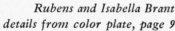

Rubens and Isabella Brant
details from color plate, page 9

PETER PAUL RUBENS

(1577–1640)

"AND SO THEY MEET, the Ionian and the Fleming, the two greatest storytellers this old earth of ours has ever borne—Homer and Rubens."

With these words, Jacob Burckhardt, himself old and great, ended his last book, the printing of which he never saw. He had called it *Erinnerungen aus Rubens* (Recollections of Rubens)—grateful remembrances of over fifty years of friendship. Rubens, one might think, should have been the last artist to fascinate the author of *The Civilization of the Renaissance in Italy* and of other works on the culture of the Mediterranean world. By what magic, we may ask, did the sensuous Fleming charm the

sober Swiss scholar? What hold had the most prominent representative of the Catholic Counter-Reformation over the heir of Calvinist severity? What attractions were offered by the painter of Baroque exuberance to the classicist for whom the Greeks and their Italian pupils of the Renaissance had formulated the ideal of beauty once and for all?

Those who see in Rubens no more than a painter of amply proportioned women and swaggering men, or a facile decorator of immense spaces in Baroque palaces and churches, will never understand how the chasm between the two worlds could ever have been bridged. Only he who penetrates

Rubens' world more deeply will find the answers to these questions. He will find that Rubens himself combined extremes in his own personality as well as in his art. He was a man of boundless vitality, yet at the same time used to strictest self-discipline. He moved with ease in the highest social circles, but he was also deeply attached to his Flemish earth and to the comforts of middle-class domesticity. He was a patriot who saw beyond the narrow limits of his own country, a statesman active in public affairs, yet at the same time a scholar thoroughly acquainted with the cultural traditions of the West.

His art, too, encompasses apparently opposite elements. For centuries he has been hailed as one of the greatest colorists, which he surely was; yet close study shows that drawing—more exactly, line—played as important a role in Rubens' art as it did in that of Raphael. He had an incomparably vivid imagination which enabled him to sketch complicated forms and actions quickly; yet he also made studies from nature throughout his life with the same loving attention to texture and detail that for

long had been the hallmark, the pride, and—in the judgment of some Italians—the limitation of Flemish art. Among his sources we find Hellenistic sculptures and Flemish primitives, Michelangelo's grand rhetoric and Caravaggio's naturalism, the sinuous bodies of the Mannerists and the brilliant color-symphonies of the Venetians.

The range of Rubens' subject matter is equally wide. He did pictures of ancient gods and heroes who come to life not as the pale shadows of philological pedantry, but as breathing, vibrant, warm-blooded human beings. There are saints who suffer the pains of martyrdom or who experience divine ecstasy, thoroughly credible in his painting no matter how strange their story. There are allegories in which scholastic personifications are built into real persons with emotional reactions common to all men. He painted portraits which give specific individuality to his models while at the same time making them typical representatives of their age, sex, or rank. Although primarily concerned with figures, human and animal, he contributed some of

STUDIES OF CATTLE, *drawing.*
From the Devonshire Collection. Reproduced by permission
The Trustees of the Chatsworth Settlement

the finest works to the category of landscape painting, works in which an abundant earth is glorified, caressed, and enveloped by the sun's warming light.

Thus, the discerning student of Rubens will find the master's work to be something very different from what it is assumed to be by popular conceptions, or misconceptions. There is bigness in Rubens, but also delicacy; strong action, but also sensitivity and lyricism. Burckhardt was right when he felt that it was a whole world that Rubens had created, and we might emphasize its *wholeness* as well as its scope. Within its enormous territory it is rich, full—and perfect. For also it has, of course, its boundaries, excluding those aspects which would disturb its perfection. The fragmentary, the irregular, the ugly had no place in it. The world of Rubens admits love and hate, exultation and suffering, life and death—but all of them whole, and with that kind of finality with which his figures are either children, or youths, or princes, or saints. It is a world of beauty in which

beauty is a function of health and vitality, not of sophistication or frailty.

There are other limitations, but—as with Homer—we do not seem to be aware of them as long as we stay within the orbit of the works themselves. Only from the outside, in the scrutiny of critical thought, do we detect the other possibilities: that Rembrandt knew of suffering deeper than any that Rubens thought of or projected; that the passing of time was caught in the quietude of Vermeer's canvases as persuasively, or more so, than in the drama and commotion of Rubens' battle-scenes; that El Greco's weird shades and flickering light were more appropriate symbols for the interpretation of the visions of Catholic mystics than Rubens' vivid and cheerful colors.

No man can do everything. Rubens—like Titian—remains a "Painter of Kings, and a King of Painters," and we are grateful for the liberal gifts which he has showered upon us.

MYSTIC MARRIAGE OF SAINT CATHERINE
Church of Saint Augustine, Antwerp

At right: THE HOLY FAMILY
Wallace Collection, London

Below: Signature of Peter Paul Rubens
Musée Plantin, Antwerp

Color plate

RUBENS AND ISABELLA BRANT

Painted 1609–1610

70½ x 53½"

Alte Pinakothek, Munich

IN MUNICH, WHERE THIS PICTURE is one of the prides of the Alte Pinakothek, it goes by the name *Die Geissblatt-Laube* (The Bower of Honeysuckle). We see the young couple in the shade of the fragrant vine: the artist, preceded by his fame abroad, had recently come home after eight years in Italy; she was the daughter of an influential and well-to-do Antwerp patrician.

They make a decorous pair in their fashionable costumes braided, embroidered, buttoned, and adorned with lace. The artist, still in his early thirties, leans towards his young wife who, sitting on the ground before him, lays her right hand trustingly on his in what looks like an accidental repetition of an age-old ceremonial gesture of marriage. Rubens' left hand lies relaxed on the hilt of his sword, but its index finger clearly points down at the joined hands, the nerve-center of the whole composition. Indeed, like Jan van Eyck's painting of the Arnolfini, this is the record of a wedding; but sacramental solemnity here has been made subordinate to informality and human warmth.

There may be a vague suggestion of hierarchy in the arrangement that gives a higher place to the man; in the position of the young woman there is indeed a faint echo of the demure maiden-saints in Flemish altarpieces of the fifteenth century. Yet we see quite well that Isabella Brant is not one of Memling's Holy Barbaras or Catharines but a young lady with an open, independent mind and even now not above the hint of a ready smile. Rubens, too, is no stern master but a gentleman who behaves towards his wife with the casual gallantry that a seventeenth-century cavalier owed to a lady. Thus, they form a union in which each partner remains an individual looking frankly at the beholder. The intimacy, the mutual trust, the tender love of the newlyweds is there, nonetheless. It is expressed by the smooth outline which ties the figures together, by the obvious parallelism and correspondence of their limbs, and by the harmonious interplay of the muted ochres, wine-reds, and dark greens.

Above: ISABELLA BRANT, *drawing British Museum, London*

At right: NUDE STUDY FOR SUSANNA AT THE BATH. *Museum, Berlin*

Color plate

THE CONVERSION OF SAINT BAVO

Painted in 1612

41½ x 65½"

National Gallery, London

STUDY FOR A CRUCIFIXION
*drawing, Boymans Museum,
Rotterdam*

FAR FROM BEING A WORK by a follower of Rubens, as some people have thought, this is one of the master's most impressive compositions. An unusually elaborate sketch, it was made for a large triptych contemplated for the Church of Saint Bavo in Ghent. The plan was never executed in this form; if it had been, the Cathedral of Ghent could boast of a work as significant for the Baroque period as its great altar by the brothers van Eyck is for the early fifteenth century.

The legend of Saint Bavo, like many similar stories of the Middle Ages, tells of a Count Allowin who upon conversion took a new name and gave away his fortune to be distributed as charity by the Church. During the Counter-Reformation the Church gave new emphasis to these stories, using them as sources of inspiration and as models for action. Yet it needed an artist like Rubens to lend life to the story, and beauty and truth.

In Rubens' plan, the main action was reserved for the central panel, with subordinated parts of the legend appearing on the narrower side-pieces. The divisions, which in the finished work would have been marked by frames, are clearly visible, but it is also evident that Rubens meant all three panels to form one grandiose unit. The layout of the stage, with its various platforms and wide staircase, and the distribution and movement of the figures are designed to lead up to the dramatic meeting of the Bishop and Count Allowin. The splendid, if archaic, costumes of the men and women, and even the handsome horses, refer to the worldly goods that the count leaves behind. The beggars and cripples at the left represent the beneficiaries of his self-sacrifice. All these figures, however, are subordinated to the magnificent architecture, the true symbol of the power of the Church whose few visible representatives dominate the scene from an elevated position.

It is, of course, a theatrical arrangement, reminiscent of large ensemble-scenes of grand opera. This is not at all accidental, since it was the period of the Baroque which developed patterns of grandeur (in building, pageantry, and even in music) which still exert their influence.

The Conversion of Saint Bavo, if finished, would have been one of the first and one of the greatest manifestations of Rubens' decorative talent. We can understand his anxiety—expressed in extant letters—to have it carried out. The sketch alone fills the eye with an almost overwhelming spectacle of color and forms in motion. At the same time, it is a work of carefully balanced relationships, for even in his grandest conceptions Rubens never forgot—and never betrayed—his classical heritage.

STUDY FOR DANIEL IN THE LION'S DEN, *drawing*
The Pierpont Morgan Library, New York

Color plate

THE ABDUCTION OF THE DAUGHTERS OF LEUCIPPUS

Painted 1615–1616

87⅜ x 82¼"

Alte Pinakothek, Munich

PAINTED IN FIGURES LARGER THAN LIFE on an almost square canvas, *The Abduction of the Daughters of Leucippus* seems at first to be primarily an exercise in composition. Four pairs of figures—the muscular twins (Castor and Pollux), the buxom women, the fiery horses, and two eager cupids—are combined into a single group that rises before us like an elaborate piece of sculpture. The eight bodies conform to a circular outline and the weights and colors are distributed in such a way that a balanced effect is achieved. Within this balance, there is a complicated use of counterpoise. One of the abductors, still astride the horse, is turning to the right, while his brother, dismounted, walks towards the left. One of them is in armor, the other nude. Of the women, one is in mid-air, her body seen frontally and in a concave pose; her sister kneels on the ground, her back curving in the opposite direction. Both of them raise their left arm and lower the right. One of the horses, a sorrel, moves towards the left foreground; the other, a gray, turns inward and rears on his hind legs. He is held by a blond cupid while a dark-haired one is associated with the darker horse. There are still subtler relationships: the youths and their horses are on the outside of the configuration so that the women are literally surrounded by them. While this arrangement effectively points up their helplessness, we are made aware also of the men's concern about the precious objects of the abduction. Men and horses form a striking background for the plaintive young women whose soft, pliant, gleaming bodies are displayed in their full nubile beauty.

This, after all, is a story of love. No matter how calculated the balance, no matter how skillful the interweaving of movements, Rubens never lost sight of the fact that abduction is one of the primeval marriage rites. The resistance of the maidens is but a token one. Their struggle is not only ineffectual, but —inadvertently or not—the hand of the upper girl glides almost caressingly over the brawny arm that lifts her up, while her sister moves more towards the man who holds and supports her, than away from him. Thus, the painting is less one of violence than one of passion, less of fear than of modesty, and the equilibrium of the design corresponds legitimately to a basic feeling of harmony. The function of the little love-gods is telling enough: they help the abductors by holding the horses' reins while their masters are occupied elsewhere. Soon they will release them, and the horses, traditional symbols of passion, will carry the couples away to a happy consummation of love.

Above and at left: details from color plate opposite

Color plate

THE LANDING OF MARIE DE MÉDICIS

Painted 1622–1623

25¼ x 19¾"

Alte Pinakothek, Munich

BETWEEN 1622 AND 1625, Rubens decorated the Luxembourg Palace in Paris with twenty-two huge paintings in honor of Marie de Médicis, the French Queen Mother. No longer in its original place, the cycle is now one of the chief attractions of the Louvre. For the big undertaking Rubens must have made many preliminary drawings and studies; only a few of them have been preserved, among them a series of color sketches in Munich from which our plate has been taken.

Even the person averse to involved ideas and erudite allusions in works of art will yet admire the lightness of touch with which the painter has suggested transparent waves and fleeting clouds, the dripping hair and glistening flesh of the figures below, and the magnificent gowns and grand poses of those above. He will be impressed by the surge of movement coming from all sides to converge upon, and to emphasize the young princess in her shining silk dress. It is a truly spectacular composition, full of action and color and glitter of light.

Yet, the painting will acquire a richer meaning for him who does not confine himself, like a gourmet of visual pleasures, to tasting its formal elements alone. The painting shows—as one in a carefully selected series of incidents—the arrival on French soil of the young Italian princess who when still a child had been engaged to the French king. The stern of the richly carved galley that has ferried her has been pushed against a landing ramp. Sailors are holding it there so that the princess and her escort may walk out from the protection of the curved roof and from under the Medici coat of arms down towards the gate of Marseilles and a canopy which is held ready for her. As the future queen of France moves forward, she receives a welcome typical of the age that exalted the monarchs into quasi godlike beings. France herself, in the form of a helmeted woman, greets her with outstretched arms. Overhead, winged Fame spreads the message of her arrival. Deities of the water, who have favored her voyage, appear like the foaming crests of surf, eager to hold and make fast the ship. The most prominent of them, three flaxen-haired nymphs, pull a rope towards and around a wooden post. Thus, allegory and mythology are called upon to join in the glorification of the ruler. Many a lesser artist, charged with similar tasks, has lost himself in pomposity and dry learning. Rubens was able to make strange happenings believable, tie together odd elements, and give to all figures such a vigorous reality that we accept them without question or astonishment.

STUDY FOR PORTRAIT OF HELENE FOURMENT
drawing, Boymans Museum, Rotterdam

Color plate

THE ARTIST'S SONS, ALBERT AND NICOLAS

Painted 1624–1625

62¼ x 32¼"

National Gallery, London

THIS PORTRAIT OF HIS TWO SONS tells us a great deal about Rubens himself. We are immediately aware of the social standing of the artist. The two boys are in costumes of fine materials replete with bows, buttons, and lacings. The billowing forms and swinging outlines of their suits are more noticeable in their ornamental effect because they are set off by the severe lines and neutral tones of an imposing architecture; yet this architecture itself adds to the impression of wealth by suggesting, as it does, a truly palatial home. The two children are clearly the sons of a man who occupies a prominent social position and who can afford what has often been called "conspicuous consumption." All the same, they are by no means solemn puppets like the children of King Charles I in one of van Dyck's most famous pictures. These are strong, healthy boys with rosy cheeks and solid Flemish bodies, quite capable of occasional mischief or a good fight.

Above all, they are unmistakably children. Not so long before Rubens, children's portraits were generally pictures of little adults, distinguished from their elders by little more than blander faces. Here we have real boys, each one recognizable as a person in his own right. Albert, the older one, perhaps ten or eleven, is acting the little gentleman, complete with hat, loose glove, and elegant crossing of legs. There is a faint trace of smugness on his face as he smiles at the beholder. The book that he holds in his right hand hints at a careful education (which, as we know, had been placed in the hands of one of Antwerp's foremost scholars). His younger brother Nicolas, about six or seven years old, watches with the frowning concentration of small children the helpless flutter of his live toy—a little bird to whose leg a string has been attached. Although Albert drapes his arm around Nicolas' shoulder as if for protection, the solid stance of the little one shows no lack of independence.

Rubens may have painted his sons at this time for another reason besides a father's pride and affection. His first born child was a girl, Clara Serena, who had died in 1623, at the age of twelve. It was probably soon after her death that Rubens decided to paint his sons, presumably some time in 1624 or 1625. The loss of one child may have made the portrayal of the surviving ones all the more meaningful. Perhaps it was the mother who wished to have such a picture. If so, she was not long permitted to enjoy it. Isabella Brant herself died soon after in 1626.

RUBENS' SON NICOLAS
drawing, Albertina, Vienna

Color plate

THE KERMESSE

Painted about 1630

58⅝ x 102¾"

The Louvre, Paris

THE PROMINENCE WHICH BRUEGEL had given to the category of "peasant painting" was not lost on Rubens, who remained a Fleming at heart, no matter how much education he absorbed or how many honors were heaped upon him. It is unlikely that any of his peasant scenes were ever expressly commissioned—which makes them all the more interesting as works of a highly personal nature.

Compared with Rubens' *Kermesse*, Bruegel's reveling peasants look static, immobile in picturesque silhouettes. Bruegel observed the life of the peasants with philosophical detachment. He noted their crude manners and vulgar appetites, but he also recognized in them the manifestation of elementary forces beyond any conventional concepts of good or evil. In Rubens' painting, we feel almost as if the earth itself had come alive in all these rolling, swaying, turbulently active bodies. There is nothing here of the standardized choreography of a country square dance. We are closer to a tribal ritual or the orgiastic abandon of an ancient bacchanal.

Strong drink and a little rustic music appear to have released what few inhibitions these people may have had. But it is also evident that all these figures, from suckling infant to tippling graybeard, are bursting with energy and are propelled by an irresistible need to convert this energy into action. Like a wedge this drinking, arguing, fighting, dancing, and embracing body of humanity is pushing out from the shaded tables of the country inn at the left towards the open fields at the right, where a few scrubby willows seem to bend under the impact of that onslaught.

We recognize in these figures the same Flemish peasants whose faces, shapes, and costumes are familiar in the works of other painters. Yet Rubens managed to give to their movements something of the rhythmic beauty of the world of animals or primitive peoples, and the whole scene is further transfigured by warm autumn colors. Indeed, we are much less conscious that these figures descend from Bruegel's yokels than that they are the distant ancestors of the ladies and gentlemen who are to people Watteau's enchanted woods.

HUNT OF WILD BOAR
Gallery, Dresden

A TREE TRUNK AND BRAMBLES, *drawing*
From the Devonshire Collection. Reproduced by permission
The Trustees of the Chatsworth Settlement

Color plate

VENUS AND ADONIS

Painted about 1635

77½ x 95¼"

The Metropolitan Museum of Art, New York

IN FRONT OF REPRODUCTIONS OF RUBENS' paintings it is well to remember the size of the originals. *Venus and Adonis*, while not large for Rubens, is many times the size of the average early Flemish painting. Pictures that big were not painted for small rooms or close inspection. The artist produced them in a spacious studio and they went into churches and palaces where they had to hold their place beside large furniture and elaborate ornament. Their bright pigments, huge bodies, and sweeping movements may overwhelm the modern beholder. In their original setting these qualities were necessary to insure the proper effect.

It would be wrong, however, to consider Rubens' works merely as part of a flamboyant system of decoration. The master had the ability to satisfy the demands for Baroque splendor without sacrificing delicate craftsmanship or thoughtful interpretation. The present painting, a good example for the truth of this statement, was painted with all the technical brilliance of Rubens' last period. Accessories are done in free, spontaneous strokes, while the figures are smoothly modeled with translucent glazes. The colors form cheerful harmonies. The gleaming flesh-color of Venus and the red and tan of Adonis stand out like the leading voices in a mellifluous operatic ensemble. They are surrounded by a festive orches-tration of yellows and greens in the landscape, grays and whites in the dogs, blues and pinks in the sky.

The subject, however, is not gay. Adonis, loved by Venus, takes leave despite her warning pleas. In his version of Ovid's tale, Rubens stressed the pathos of a woman who knows that her lover goes to his death. With real feeling he painted Venus' moist eyes, trying to absorb forever the familiar features, and her beautiful arms and hands which seem to caress while they restrain the hunter. He added, too, the delightful touch of Cupid holding on with child-ish eagerness to the brawny leg of the big man, and he painted Adonis calming what appears to him the unreasonable anxiety of a loving woman.

Rubens left no doubt that the urge to hunt will prevail over the woman's attractions. The bodies of the lovers form an almost regular pyramid in the center of the picture. Yet there is no stability in this design. Strong diagonals, from the body of Venus to the raised arm of Adonis, and from the wooded knoll at the right to the open distance at the left, indicate that the youth will go where his sleek hounds are pointing, and where he will meet his fate. If Rubens avoided emphasizing the somber mood of the story it was, perhaps, because he knew also its end. After his death, Adonis was transformed into a flower, the beautiful anemone.

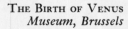

THE BIRTH OF VENUS
Museum, Brussels

Color plate

ALLEGORY OF WAR

Painted about 1637

81⅛ x 134⅝″

Pitti Palace, Florence

IF THERE ARE PEOPLE WHO think that modern interpreters read too much into old paintings, they might do well to examine the letter which Rubens sent in 1638 to Florence to explain one of his pictures shipped there shortly before. It was the famous *Allegory of War*, still admired as one of the greatest of the master's late works. This is what Rubens wrote:

"The principal figure is Mars who has left the temple of Janus open (which according to Roman custom remained closed in time of peace) and struts with his shield and his bloodstained sword, threatening all peoples with disaster; he pays little attention to Venus, his lady, who, surrounded by her little love-gods, tries in vain to hold him back with caresses and embraces. On the opposite side, Mars is pulled forward by the Fury Alecto with a torch in her hand. There are also monsters signifying plague and famine, the inseparable companions of war. Thrown to the ground is a woman with a broken lute, as a symbol that harmony cannot exist beside the discord of war; likewise a mother with a child in her arms indicates that fertility, procreation, and tenderness are opposed by war, which breaks into and destroys everything. There is furthermore an architect fallen backwards, with his tools in his hands, to express the idea that what is built in peace for the benefit and ornament of cities is laid in ruin and razed by the forces of arms. I believe, if I remember rightly, that you will also find on the ground, beneath the feet of Mars, a book and a drawing on paper, to indicate that he tramples on literature and other refinements. There ought to be also a bundle of arrows or spears, with the thong for binding them together loosened; for when bound together they are the emblem of concord. Likewise, thrown aside, are also the caduceus and the olive, the symbols of peace. The sorrowing woman, however, clothed in black with a torn veil, and deprived of all her jewels and ornaments is unhappy Europe which for so many years has suffered pillage, degradation, and misery affecting all of us so deeply that it is useless to say more about them. Her symbol is the globe with a cross on top, which is carried by a small angel or Genius, the sign of the Christian world."

We are fortunate in having Rubens' own explanation of all these details. Even without it, however, we could not miss the main theme of the picture. It is dominated by an irresistible movement towards the gloomy and foreboding area at the right. Nothing avails against the forces of war once they are set into motion. The theme of the Venus and Adonis picture has here been developed into a message of universal significance, one that has lost none of its power and none of its truth.

STUDIES OF HEADS AND HANDS
drawing, Albertina, Vienna

SUSANNE FOURMENT
(LE CHAPEAU DE PAILLE)

Painted about 1622

30¼ x 21"

National Gallery, London

LANDSCAPE
WITH RAINBOW

Painted 1635–1638

53¼ x 92"

Wallace Collection, London

ON HIS TRIP TO THE NETHERLANDS in 1781 Sir Joshua Reynolds saw a painting which he described as "an admirable portrait by Rubens known by the name *Chapeau de Paille*. . . . It has a wonderful transparency of color as if seen in the open air; it is upon the whole a very striking portrait; but her breasts are as ill drawn as they are finely colored." Most people will agree with Reynolds' praise while not necessarily accepting his censure. The most puzzling thing about the picture has always been its name *Chapeau de Paille* which already in Reynolds' time was traditional. It has caused many learned discussions, since in modern usage *paille* means straw, while the hat in the painting is evidently of felt. Recently, however, it has been pointed out that *paille* once had also the meaning of "dais." The hat in the portrait functions indeed like a canopy. Since standing or walking under a canopy was one of the privileges of princes, the title may indicate a subtle flattery. It could, however, also contain a reference to the canopy of marriage ceremonies. Rubens' model was Susanne Fourment, who married (for a second time) in 1622. The painting could very well date from this period, when she was twenty-three.

It is easy to see that Rubens painted this portrait *con amore*. The billowing forms of the costume, neutral in tone save for one strong red, emphasize the smooth, luminous, subtly shaded colors of the flesh. The blue sky lends outdoor freshness, rendering all the more attractive the young lady whose pose is so modest and whose expression so alluring.

We cannot know what went on in Rubens' mind when he painted this picture, and whether the inspired state in which he must have worked was due only to artistic enthusiasm. It is, however, worth remembering that he not only painted Susanne's portrait more than once, but that after the death of his first wife he married her younger sister, the sixteen-year-old Helene Fourment.

WHEN THE ROMANTIC PAINTER turned to nature he looked for solace and solitude. Not so Rubens. His landscapes are the setting for many useful or diverting activities. Moreover, nature herself is "agitated" in his pictures. Wind and weather, light and shadow play across the fertile fields, the brooks and ponds, the grasses and the trees.

The landscape in the Wallace Collection is a good example of this approach. From its broad expanse there rises a warming sensation of contentment and well-being. A brief summer rain has cleared the air, though shadows from clouds are still lurking in some sections. With its sweeping embrace, a glittering rainbow reaches from one side of the picture to the other. Below, the eye follows the gentle directives of various diagonals until it reaches the bluish zone where earth and sky melt into one.

Man and beast follow their normal tasks and inclinations. The sociable farm hands at the left, the cattle in the center, the preening and fluttering ducks at the right give life to each section of the picture. A few gay touches of red, blue, and white enliven the prevailing ochres of the fields and the greens of the trees. Everything conveys to us the joy with which Rubens beheld creation. The deeply religious master saw in nature the work of God, and he communicates to us the happiness that filled him whenever he looked at it.

AN ALMOST NUDE MAN, *drawing*
Courtesy Her Royal Highness
The Princess Wilhelmina
of the Netherlands